Dedication

This book is dedicated to my children, Joel, Brooke, Melody, & Chucky, from whom I receive my best writing material. Thank you for all the *drama*. May every dream that God places within you come true.

Look Mom, no hands! Is this what you meant by *let go and let God*? Mom, you've inspired me through your grace, and you have encouraged me through your life & your words. You're my biggest cheerleader & my biggest fan. Thank you for the gifts in me that you help to refine. Thank you for being my BFF, but most of all, I thank you for teaching me about God, and making sure I knew all about my loving Savior, Jesus Christ. That is the best gift any parent could ever give. Mom, you really are *the bestest*. I love you.

Thank you Pastor Greg & Tammy Cooper for encouraging me in the art of puppetry & enriching my life with God's word & wisdom. May people see the works of a loving, living, & giving Savoir when they look upon your smiling faces.

All thanks and praise and glory be to the most high God for saving me & allowing me, with all my quirks and flaws, to be used in this humbling way to help win the lost. I love you, Jesus.

Contents

What's inside?

Puppet skits: Several reproducible puppet skits to choose from to fit your needs. Skits consist of 2-4 puppets each. Every skit focuses on salvation through Jesus Christ, God's love for us, peace through Christ, & how very precious we are to our loving heavenly Father who created us, & created all for us.

Lessons: Along with the skits, there will be a handful of lesson plans. Each Lesson brings the message of Jesus to children & adults alike. Upbeat interactive sermons convey God's love through His word. Each lesson is written so that a person who has never heard of Jesus before can easily understand who He is & what He has done for them.

Leader Tips: Whether you are setting up in a local park or traveling overseas, there is a lot of planning to do. Simplify the process by taking full advantage of the tips & resources included in this book.

Object Lessons: Lessons that contain objects, illustrations, & visual aides to help express the message with a visually dramatic presence.

Great Commission Crafts: Crafts that serve as a witnessing tool! They'll learn more about Jesus while making the craft, & then they'll take what they make with them as not only a reminder of God's love but as a tool to help them tell others about Jesus!

Dear Beloved,

If you are reading this now, you are more than likely preparing to make history. That's right. You, my friend, are getting ready to change the future. What you are getting ready to do will go down in the book! Every new name written into "The Book of Life" will change the future of God's kingdom for eternity!

You can get so busy preparing for the big event that you may forget that you are right smack in the middle of storming the gates of hell. You are in the midst of a battle. It's war! Ephesians 6:12 says, "For our struggle is not against flesh & blood, but against the rulers, against the authorities, against the powers of this dark world & against the spiritual forces of evil in the heavenly realms." The enemy is not just going to let you waltz into his camp & free all the prisoners-of-war without a fight!

If you are a leader, remember to lead in love. All of us are accountable to somebody, so let's put away our pride & submit. After all, even David was obedient as he submitted to that one crazy spear-throwing king. Don't forget that when David was the target of all that spear throwing, he never called up his buddies on the phone to "vent" about his mad king. He never took to gossiping. Don't let anything get in the way of the goal. Winning souls is the goal. The devil is going to try every trick in the book to tear down relationships & do whatever he can to come between you & the goal. I mention gossiping because it is so prevalent in the church today. God detests it. In Romans 1:28-32 God refers to gossips in the same way He depicts murderers & God-haters. When you decide to partake in gossiping or *choose* not to be obedient to your leader, you send an open invitation to the prideful spirit of rebellion. God's Word tells us in 1 Samuel 15:23, "For rebellion is as the sin of witchcraft, & stubbornness is as iniquity & idolatry." Don't invite the enemy into your camp. Keep him out of your camp, & you go make a mess of his! We have got to stop giving the enemy permission to attack us. "When you are encamped against your enemies, keep away from everything impure." Deuteronomy 23:9.

Prepare yourselves. Pray together & fast together. Above all else, love one another. We need to love as Christ loved the church (John 13:34) & honor one another above ourselves (Romans 12:10). Let's commit ourselves to stop & think before we speak, act, or react. We need to ask ourselves, "Would I want somebody talking about or treating me this way?" Jesus said this is how the world would know we belonged to Him, simply by loving one another.

With all that said, the only thing left to say is I love you, & I have been praying for you for quite some time now.

Love in Christ,

Andriea Irene Chenot
www.PuppetsForJESUS.com

Skits

The One Way to Heaven

Brooke: *(enters alone)* This is just great. What is the point of me being on time if he is always late? Helloooo? Hel looooo?

Melody: *(enters)* Hello. Are you calling me?

Brooke: No. I was not calling you, Melody. I was calling Joel. He is late. As always.

Melody: Nobody is perfect.

Brooke: Well I'm pretty close, but I'm a rare exception. So, quit wasting time & help me call Joel.

Melody: I didn't mean to waste time. I don't try to waste anything.

Brooke: Sometimes I feel like I am wasting my breath.

Melody: *(sweetly & innocently)* Maybe you shouldn't talk so much. That could help you save your breath.

Joel: *(enters)* I can agree with that! Why don't you quit talking so much, Brooke? Save your breath!

Brooke: Why don't you try being on time.

Joel: I tried it… once.

Melody: We are all here except Chucky.

Chucky: *(enters)* Here I am!

Melody: Chucky! I am so glad you are here. Now we can introduce everybody.

Chucky: Allow me!

Melody: Go for it little bro!

Chucky: This is our big brother Joel.

Joel: The one & only!

Brooke: Thank goodness for that!

Chucky: And that would be our big sister Brooke.

Brooke: I might not be the oldest, but I am definitely the smartest.

Joel: Just ask her, she'll tell ya.

Chucky: This is my big sister Melody. She's just a little bit older than me, but I love Jesus just as much as she does!

Melody: That would be me!

Chucky: And I'm Chucky!

Brooke: Let's quit wasting time & do what we came here to do.

Joel: Speaking of wasting, why are you still wasting your breath?

Brooke: Speaking of breath, why does yours always stink?

Joel: Maybe it's yours. Your breath is closer to your nose than mine is.

Brooke: Joel!

Chucky: Uh oh. Here they go again.

Melody: We are here to tell everybody how to get to heaven.

Joel: When I grow up, I am going to be an astronaut & fly to heaven.

Brooke: Why wait until then? Why not hike a ride to the moon right now?

Chucky: There is only one way to heaven.

Melody: Jesus is the only way to heaven. By accepting Jesus into your heart, you can live with Him in heaven for eternity.

Brooke: Eternity means forever & ever & ever.

Joel: I feel like you have been talking for eternity.

Chucky: To go to heaven, all you have to do is ask Jesus to come into your heart & forgive you of your sins.

Brooke: Sin is the bad stuff that you do or say. Personally, I think Joel's bad breath should be a sin.

Joel: You're smelling something closer to your nose.

Brooke: I never!

Joel: You never shut up!

Melody: Sin can be unkind words that you say to somebody else like YOUR BROTHER or YOUR SISTER.

Brooke: Sorry Joel.

Joel: Sorry Sis.

Chucky: That's better!

Melody: Just remember, if you want to go to heaven, & you are really sorry for your sins, all you have to do is ask Jesus to forgive you & He will wash all your sins away.

Chucky: Jesus will make you brand new! He not only forgives your sins, He totally forgets them too!

Brooke: I am so exceptionally smart that I never forget anything.

Joel: Yep. She's smart. Just ask her. She'll tell ya.

Melody: We better go before they go at it again.

Chucky: Good idea Sis.

Joel, Brooke, Melody, & Chucky: BYE!!! *(exit)*

Don't forget the tracts!

Make use of every second of your trip! Be sure to pick up plenty of tracts. We recommend American Tract Society. On average, tracts cost about 10 cents each. With many languages to choose from in addition to a great wealth of topics for every age group, an online visit to the American Tract Society is a must before any missions trip.

- Stock everyone in your group with plenty of tracts.

- Buy tracts in the native language of the place you will be traveling.

- Study the false religions in the area & buy tracts on that topic

- Purchase an assortment of tracts for all age groups

www.atstracts.org

Do everything without complaining or arguing so that you may become blameless and pure, children of God without fault in a crooked and depraved generation, in which you shine like stars in the universe. Philippians 2:14-15 ☆

Peace That Passes Understanding

Melody: *(enters singing with high energy)* I got the joy joy joy joy down in my heart. I got the peace that passes understanding…

Chucky: Peace passes understanding? Where's the race? Vroooooooom!

Melody: *(giggling)* A race! Peace & understanding racing? That is silly! Teee heeee heeee!

Chucky: Well big sister, that is what YOU were singing. *(singing)* "I have the peace that PASSES understanding!" Who is peace? Who is understanding? Those are some weird names.

Melody: *(laughing)* Yeah, those would be some funny names! You're too funny!

Chucky: I'm not the one who was singing about the race. You were. *(singing)* I got the peace that passes understanding…

Melody: Now I get it! That is what I was singing about. The peace that passes all understanding. I have the love of Jesus in my heart.

Chucky: Melody, you are one of the happiest girls I know!

Melody: That is the Love Jesus. Once you accept Jesus, He comes into your life & brings joy & peace. The peace Jesus gives us is so wonderful that it is hard to understand. It is peace beyond understanding.

Chucky: Ohhh, now I get it. Hey! I've got an idea. Why don't we tell everyone about Jesus.

Melody: Great idea little bro! Everybody listen up. Jesus is God's one & only Son. I am talking about the one & only true God. The God that created the whole world. The earth, the sun, the moon, the sky, God created it all! God even made you. God loves you more than you will ever know. He wants good things for you. The Bible tells us that God made you & He has prepared a purpose & plan for your life before you were even born! All you have to do is accept Jesus to start living the life of joy & peace that God has planned for you.

Chucky: What about sin? Don't forget to tell them about sin. Sin is anything bad that we do or say.

Melody: That is why we all need Jesus. The Bible tells us that we have all sinned. We have all done things that were wrong at one time or another, but Jesus never sinned or did anything wrong.

Chucky: Jesus died on a cross for the sins of the world.

Melody: Yep, Jesus died for all of you because He loves you so much. You are so precious to Him. He loves you so much that if any one of you were the only person on earth, He would have still died just for you.

Chucky: How about the big bad sins? Does Jesus forgive the big sins or just the little ones?

Melody: It does not matter how big, how bad, or how many. Jesus forgives all sins. There is nothing you can do that Jesus will not forgive. If you really want to change & live for God then Jesus will wash away every bad thing that you have ever done. He forgives it all, & He totally forgets it forever. All you have to do is ask Him, & turn away from those old ways.

Chucky: Everybody needs Jesus!

Melody: You've got that right little bro.

Chucky & Melody: *(exit singing)* I got the joy joy joy joy down in my heart! I got the peace that passes understanding...

Pack light & leave lighter!

Consider what puppets you will be taking with you. You want lightweight puppets that pack & travel well. However, you do not want to sacrifice quality or size. For this, we highly recommend Puppet Revelation puppets. Puppet Revelation is a Christian company who crafted these puppets with missions in mind.

You can find Puppet Revelation puppets at www.PuppetsForJESUS.com - Be sure to call in your order, & let them know that your puppets are being used for missions. They are already the low price leader in the industry, but they give additional discounts to all products purchased for missions.

If you are traveling to an area that is financially challenged, consider leaving behind a good portion of the materials that you will be using while you are there. Because of your willingness, ministry through puppets can continue long after you are gone.

www.PuppetsForJESUS.com also offers a lightweight portable puppet stage that easily collapses & expands. Try to avoid dealing with the traditional PVC stage if at all possible. There are better ways to use your time. The collapsible stage weighs a light 20 pounds & comes in a nice canvas duffle bag that can be one of your carry-on pieces with most airlines. Remember to place your order by phone for additional savings & benefits.

For Those Who Hurt

Chucky & Melody: *(enter together)*

Melody: I have some good news! In fact, it is the best news ever! It is the greatest news of all! Jesus loves you! That's right! Jesus loves you so very much!

Chucky: I know you're right sis, but sometimes I wonder.

Melody: What do you mean Chucky?

Chucky: Well I wonder why Jesus or God would let anything bad happen to people.

Melody: That is a good question Chucky.

Chucky: Some kids seem to have it so hard.

Melody: I know Chucky. Sometimes the people that should be the ones to love & protect us are the ones that hurt us the most. Sometimes it might seem like we haven't got a friend in the world. Sometimes life can get hard.

Chucky: But why would God let that happen to anyone that He loves?

Melody: Jesus loves us more than anything. He would never hurt us. Other PEOPLE may hurt us; even people who we thought were our friends can hurt us. Sometimes, our own family can be the ones who hurt us most.

Chucky: Why would God let people hurt other people?

17

Melody: God never wants anyone to be hurt, but God does not force anybody to choose one way or another. God gave people minds & He allows people to make their own choices, even bad choices, if that is what somebody decides to do. We all make CHOICES. Sometimes people make bad choices that hurt other people. Sometimes people make choices that hurt us. God never hurts us, but other people sometimes do.

Chucky: Why would people be so mean & uncaring?

Melody: The Bible says in 1 John 4:8 that people are this way because they do not know God. God is love & everything good, & if you don't know God then you can't truly love anybody because God is the love inside of us. God is love.
Chucky: So when somebody mistreats me it is because they don't have Jesus in their heart? It is because they do not know God?

Melody: That's right Chucky.

Chucky: It seems like some kids have it tougher than anyone. What would you tell them?

Melody: *(address the audience)* Let me tell everybody this. God has a purpose & plan for every one of you. He has a job that only you can do. If it seems like a lot of bad stuff has happened to you in your life, & you have been hurt a lot, it is because the devil knows that the purpose & plan that God has for your life is so big & so wonderful that he is going to try to destroy you any way he can.

Chucky: Okay, let me get this straight. The devil wants to destroy people because of God's plan?

Melody *(to the audience)* Yes! The devil knows that you are going to do great big things for God because God has had great big things planned for your life before you were even born. This scares the devil because the devil knows that a lot of people are going to get to know Jesus just because of you. The devil doesn't want this to happen so he is trying to put a stop to it. He uses the people in your life that don't know Jesus to hurt you so you will turn against God.

Chucky: *(address the audience)* Wow, I never looked at it that way before. How exciting! You are going to make a big difference for God's kingdom! God wants to use you! God has big plans for your life! God loves you sooooo much!

Melody: He sure does! God knows you'll have hard & difficult times, but He will be there with you. He will always see you through. God will not let anything or anyone destroy you. As long as you keep praying & obeying God, you will make it through. You may still have hard times, but you will make it through them, & God will use you to make a big difference for His kingdom.

Chucky: I am going to keep praying & obeying God. I am going to do all I can to follow God & all His ways so I will be ready to do whatever it is that God has planned for me to do.

Melody: That is exactly what you should do. Keep praying. God listens! Continue to obey God, & keep learning about God every way that you can. Trust in God because He loves you more than you could ever know.

Chucky: I love God toooooo. He makes me happy happy happy.

Melody: I know you love God. It is easy to see by the way you love other people.

Chucky: Yep, God is the love inside of me! I'm going to go share God's love with everybody that I know!

Melody & Chucky: Bye everybody!

Royalty

Melody & Brooke: *(enter together)*

Melody: Joel & Chucky should be here soon. I can't wait!

Brooke: Well you'll probably have to because Joel is always late.

Melody: We all have things we can improve on.

Brooke: Speak for yourself. It would be rather difficult to improve on perfection. Anyways, while we are waiting, I will let you in on a little secret. Guess what?

Joel: *(enters)* What? You still suck your thumb?

Brooke: Joel! UGHHH!

Melody: Where's Chucky?

Chucky: *(enters quickly)* Here I am!

Melody: There you are! Brooke was just getting ready to let us in on a little secret.

Brooke: You can forget it now that he is here.

Joel: Let me guess. You mean me?

Brooke: Gee, you're swift.

Chucky: Aww, come on Brooke.

Melody: Yeah, tell us.

Brooke: Okay. Guess what?

Joel: So do you?

Brooke: Do I what?

Joel: Still suck your thumb?

Brooke: No!

Chucky: You put a bean in your nose?

Brooke: No!

Chucky: You pick your nose?

Melody: *(giggling)* You're so silly chucky.

Chucky: Well she said to guess.

Melody: I didn't really want you to guess.

Chucky: Then why did you say, "Guess what?"

Melody: Because I wanted you to ask what.

Joel: Then why not just say ask what instead of guess what? I wish girls would just say what they mean. I just don't get it

Brooke: You never get it!

Chucky: Get what? If somebody is passing out candy, I want to get some of that!

Brooke: Forget it! I'll just tell you. Sometimes, I imagine that a royal prince comes to take me away to his beautiful kingdom. I pretend I am a princess. Do you think I look like a princess?

Chucky: Do you think I look like a frog?

Melody: You're silly, Chucky!

Chucky: That reminds me of what I learned in Sunday school. You don't have to pretend to be a princess. You do not have to imagine a prince coming to take you away to his wonderful kingdom. That is really going to happen. You are already a princess too.

Joel: She reminds me more of the toad in the story.

Brooke: Be quiet! Joel the TROLL!

Melody: I think the troll is in a different story.

Chucky: You're right Melody. No trolls or toads in this story. Actually, this isn't any ordinary story. This is a true story about a true prince. This story is about a real King.

Melody: Now you are just being silly again.

Joel: I think Brooke looks silly!

Brooke: Well I oughtta!!

Joel: I agree. You oughtta. You oughtta shut your yap.

Melody: Uh oh. Chucky, please tell us about the TRUE story before they get us kicked out of here.

Chucky: Jesus is God's one & only Son. Jesus is the King of Kings & Lord of Lords. God is your heavenly Father right?

Melody: Of course He is. God made us, & God made the whole world for us.

Chucky: Well if God is the mightiest of all kings, & He is your Father, what does that make you?

Melody: That makes me a princess! I am royalty.

Chucky: That's right!

Brooke: Well what about my prince? Will a prince really come for me?

Joel: Not if he's smart.

Chucky: Yes, Brooke. The Prince will come for you. Jesus is the Prince of Peace. Jesus is God's one & only Son. Jesus left His home in Heaven & came to earth to die for our sins. Jesus died on the cross for our sins so that all who accept him can be forgiven, washed clean, made new, & set free! After Jesus died on the cross & took our punishment for our sins, He came back to life! Not even death could hold Jesus down! He is so mighty & powerful, & He loves us so so so so sooo much.

And, before Jesus left the earth to return to His kingdom in Heaven, He told us that He was going to prepare a place for us in Heaven, & after He was done He would come back for us & take us with Him.

Melody: That's right! I read that in my Bible. God's Word tells us that without Jesus no one can go to Heaven. Once you accept Jesus as your Lord & Savior, you become a child of The Most High God! You belong to a royal kingdom!

Chucky: My Father is the King above all Kings! He made all of the earth & He made it just for me! He is the Beginning & He is the End, but best of all, He is my dearest friend!

Melody: I am going to go read my Bible & wait for my prince. He might not come today, but I want to be ready if He does!

Chucky: That's right! Jesus is coming back real soon! Only God knows the day & the hour, but the Bible tells us to be ready, because He is coming for us soon!

Joel, Brooke, Melody, & Chucky: Bye everybody! *(exit)*

The Rapture

Joel & Chucky: *(enter)*

Joel: That sister of yours! She is always talking about me being late, but now here I am waiting on her! UGHH! That sister of yours!

Chucky: She's your sister too.

Joel: Don't remind me.

Brooke: *(enter)* Don't remind you? Don't remind you of what? You need to be reminded of everything. You don't even chew your food without somebody reminding you. Brothers!

Melody: *(enter)* Everybody needs to be reminded of something every now & then.

Joel: Well I was on my way to the movies & now I missed my bus! I am going to miss out on the best show ever!

Chucky: Return of the space monsters!

Brooke: Yeah, Joel was in that movie.

Melody: Really?

Brooke: Yeah, he was the slimy one.

Joel: Hardee har har. I'm not laughing. I missed the bus, & now I will miss out on the best movie of all times.

Brooke: More like the dumbest movie of all times.

Joel: The best!

Brooke: Dumbest!

Joel: Best!

Brooke: Dumbest!

Joel: Best!

Chucky: Well you can still see it. It is playing every few hours at the theatre, right?

Melody: Yeah, & you can catch the next bus.

Chucky: Yeah. You can catch the next bus. It is not like you missed the rapture or anything.

Brooke: Really! It is not like Jesus just came back & you were left behind or something.

Melody: Jesus said that He would be coming back for us.

Brooke: Nobody except God knows the day or hour that Jesus will return. You can check the newspaper to see when your movie is playing again.

Chucky: Yeah, but if you're not ready when Jesus comes, there is not going to be a next show.

Melody: You got that right, little brother. Jesus is going to come in the sky.

Chucky: Everyone all over the entire earth will be able to see Him coming.

Melody: Everybody will be able to hear the trumpet blast from heaven too.

Chucky: And then in a blink of an eye, everybody that belongs to Jesus will be gone!

Melody: They will be in Heaven with Jesus! It will be the best day ever!

Joel: Yeah for those who are ready. But for the ones who have not accepted Jesus, it will be the worst day ever.

Brooke: Well as long as you have accepted Jesus into your heart, you don't have to worry. You can look forward to meeting Jesus in the sky!

Joel: I was looking forward to The Return of the Space Monsters, but even the best movie of all times will not compare to Jesus coming back!

Melody: I can't wait!

Chucky: Me either!

Joel: Hey, here comes the next bus! We can all see the Space Monster movie.

Brooke: I have already seen one.

Joel: You've seen the first one?

Brooke: No.

Joel: What one are you talking about then?

Brooke: The slimy one. Gotta go! *(exit)*

Joel: Brooke! *(exit)*

Melody: Keep obeying God & be ready! *(exit)*

Chucky: Jesus is coming back real soon! *(exit)*

My Favorite Color

You will need: 1 piece each of the following colors of construction paper: black, red, white, blue, green, & gold.

Here's what ya do: Choose six kids & give them each one of the six colors of paper. Have them sit on the floor in front of the audience. Every time their color is mentioned by one of the puppets, instruct them to stand up & hold their color high above their head & immediately sit back down. Make sure you tell them that they must quickly stand & sit every single time their color is mentioned. After the skit is over, allow them to take a big bow before returning to their seats.

♥ ♥ ♥ ♥ ♥ ♥ ♥ ♥

Melody & Chucky: *(enter)*

Chucky: Hey Mellie, what did you get in your Snappy Meal? I got a mini sports racer, & it's red! My favorite color!

Melody: I got a blue ballerina. I already have four of those, blue, blue, blue, blue, blue. I wanted a pink one. Pink is my favorite color. I would color my whole world pink if I could. Pink sky, pink clouds, pink grass, pink trees, pink, pink, pink! I just looooove pink!

Chucky: Wow. You really do love pink! I learned that pink is just red with a little white mixed in.

Melody: Hey, you're right, little bro, just like green & yellow make blue.

Chucky: I wonder what Joel's & Brooke's favorite colors are. Green? Blue? Black? I think Joel likes sporty black. Gold? Pink? Or should I say red with white? Is white even really a color? White is a tricky one. What do you think sis, is white a color?

Melody: *(giggles)* Yes, white is a color. You have white paint don't ya? White crayons, white clouds, & even the white eggshell has white egg whites inside of them. So yes, white is definitely a color.

Chucky: I think you are right. You are right about white! White is a color. I still wonder what Joel's & Brooke's favorite colors are.

Melody: I don't know. Why don't we ask them.

Chucky: *(call Joel)* Joel, excuse me, Joel. Are you there?

Joel: *(enter)* Here I am. The one & only!

Brooke: *(enter)* Thank goodness for that.

Joel: For what?

Brooke: That there is only one of you, Mr. One & Only.

Joel: I am just going to ignore that.

Brooke: Like you ignored Mom when she told you to put on deodorant?

Joel: Maybe you ignored your toothbrush & you're smelling your own bad breath.

Brooke: Joel!

Chucky: Hey guys, aren't you forgetting something?

Brooke: Yeah, Joel forgot his deodorant.

Joel: Brooke forgot to brush!

Melody: Noooooo. Are you forgetting that we are in front of an audience, & Mom told us to be on our best behavior?

Joel: Oh yeah, right. Ooops. So what did you call us out here for anyways.

Chucky: We wanted to know what your favorite color was.

Brooke: Mine is gold. Shiny shiny gold. Gold! Gold! Gold!

Joel: Mine is Black! Jet black. Fassssst black! Like sports car black. Slick black!

Melody: Hey. That reminds me of a story. Joel's favorite color, black, is where it all begins.

Chucky: I think I know where you are going with this. Brooke's favorite color, Gold, is where the story ends. Well actually, it never ends.

Melody: That's right little bro!

Brooke: I know exactly what you two are talking about, & if you are going to tell this story, you have got to do it right. Since I am obviously the smartest, I will take charge here.

Joel: *(sarcastically)* Yeah. She's the smartest alright. Just ask her, she'll tell ya.

Brooke: *(put strong emphasis on "read")* Who read, that's right, read, & read, & read, & read, 102 books this summer? Me, that is who. I even took notes with my red pen. My teacher always corrects papers with her read pen, but when I do reports on the books I read, she never has to use her red pen on my papers. So, since I read the most, & take notes with my red pen, & my teacher never has to use her red pen on my work, I would say that makes me the smartest, & the most qualified to be in charge here. So without any further ado, let us begin. Read-y? Good. Let's go. Black is the darkest color of all. Sin is also dark. Sin is anything bad that you do or say.

Melody: Like being mean, lying, or disobeying your parents.

Chucky: The Bible tells us that we all have sinned.

Brooke: That is correct. Everyone has sinned. Everyone except Jesus.

Joel: Can you believe that Jesus left His home in heaven & came to earth to die for our sins?

Brooke: I believe it, & it's true. The color red represents the blood of Jesus.

Melody: Jesus is God's one & only son who died on the cross for our sins.

Chucky: Jesus isn't dead anymore though.

Brooke: Correct again. Jesus is alive!

Joel: Yeah, he is in heaven with God, & if you want to go to heaven then all you have to do is accept Jesus as your Lord & Savior.

Brooke: Yes, even Joel knows that.

Melody: Once you accept Jesus, He washes all those sins away. He takes what was once black & dark in your heart & makes it white as snow.

Chucky: God not only forgives your sins, He totally forgets them too!

Brooke: Again, I must say that you are correct. I have obviously taught you well.

Joel: You keep thinking that.

Brooke: I plan on it.

Melody: After you accept Jesus & your sins are washed away, you need to be baptized with water.

Brooke: Blue is the color of water.

Chucky: Speaking of water, God wants to pour out His Holy Spirit upon you like water.

Melody: God wants to fill you up with His Holy Spirit.

Joel: The Holy Spirit makes you brave & gives you courage!

Melody: The Holy Spirit comforts you & gives you peace.

Brooke: And that brings us to green.

Joel: Green will be the color of your teeth if you don't brush them.

Brooke: I do brush!

Joel: Says who?

Brooke: Says me.

Chucky: Green means that we keep growing as Christians. We grow & we change.

Melody: That's right little bro. We don't do that same old stuff that we used to do, like fighting with our brothers & sisters.

Chucky: Right Brooke?

Brooke: *(humbled)* Right.

Melody: Right Joel?

Joel: *(humbled)* Right, Sis.

Brooke: Hey, that brings us to the end, my favorite color, Gold! Gold represents heaven in all of its splendor & glory. Nobody is ever sad or blue in heaven.

Joel: The streets are made of gold in heaven, & Jesus is going to place a gold crown on our heads. Talk about your bling-bling!

Chucky: And the story never ends!

Melody: Because we will live forever & ever in heaven with Jesus!!

Joel, Brooke, Melody, & Chucky: *(cheer, praise, shout halleluiah & exit)*

Lessons

Color Me His!

Black: This is the sin on your heart. Sin is all the bad stuff that you ever did. The Bible says that we have all sinned. The Bible also tells us that the punishment for your sin is death, but God's gift is a life that lasts forever through Christ Jesus. (Romans 3:23, Romans 6:23)

Red: This is the price that was paid for your sins. God loves you so much that He sent His one & only Son, Jesus to die on the cross for your sins. Jesus took the punishment for your sins so you would not have to. Jesus is the only way to Heaven. Red represents the Blood of Jesus Christ that was shed for your sins. (Romans 5:8)

White: When you accept Jesus as your Lord & Savior, all your sins will be forgiven. You are made brand new. All your sins are gone forever, & you are washed clean. (2 Corinthians 5:17)

Blue: After we accept Jesus we are baptized with water. This is symbolizes our commitment to God before man that we are washing away our old ways & we are now a new creature in Christ.

God loves you so much that He wants to pour out His Spirit on you like water. God said that His Spirit is not just for adults, but it is for children too. God's Word says that His Spirit will fill you up so God can use you for His work. God's Spirit will bring you comfort & peace. God's Spirit will protect you from harm. God's Spirit will give you power, strength, courage, wisdom, & boldness to serve God in a mighty powerful way. (Acts 2:17, John 3:5)

Green: Just like a plant grows from a seed, your relationship with God must grow too. Today is just the start of your journey with the one true God. Remember, God is your Father in heaven, He created you & He wants to get closer to you so that you can grow closer to him. We do this by learning about Him through His Word the Bible, & also by praying & talking to Him. God is your creator. He made you, & He is your Father who loves you, but He is also your dearest friend. God waits for you to talk to Him. When you learn about Him through the Bible, & talk to Him through prayer, He will come closer to you, & your spirit will grow in the goodness of God. (2 Peter 3:18, James 4:8, John 4:23)

Gold: One day you will walk with Jesus on streets of Gold! When your life on earth is done, your life that lasts forever will begin. You will live forever in Heaven where there is no more pain, no suffering, no sorrow, or hurt. There will only be peace, joy, & love in Heaven. Jesus is there right now preparing your place. He promises to come back for us so that we can live forever with Him! (John 3:16, Revelation 21:21, John 14:2)

Prepare for your altar call. Allow time for the Holy Spirit to come & have His way in your service. Allow ample time for the Spirit to move.

God's Gift

God loves you more than anything that you could ever imagine. But since God is holy, sin separates us from God. God's holiness means that He is all good, all love, totally pure, with not even a drop of anything bad. God is absolutely perfect. This is why our sin separates us from God. Sin is any bad thing that we have ever done, thought, said, or told somebody else to do. Sin is lying, cheating, hurting others, & disobeying God. The Bible tells us in Romans 3:23 that everybody has sinned, each & every one of us. Me, you, & everyone that ever lived except God's only Son, Jesus. The Bible also tells us in Romans 6:23 That the wages of sin is death, but the gift of GOD is eternal life through CHRIST JESUS our Lord. The first part of that verse means that we all deserve to be punished by death & be separated from God forever because of our sins. This is what we deserve, & this is what our punishment should be. We do not deserve to ever go to heaven. But the good news is that God loves us so much that there is a second part to that verse, & we will talk about that later.

God's Gift Object Lesson

You Will Need: One big empty box wrapped as a gift (the bigger the better) & one helper.

Leader is the person that is giving the message
Helper The person giving the gift

Helper: *(runs up to the leader very excitedly with the gift)* Look! Look! I have something for you. It's a gift! I couldn't wait to give it to you

Leader: Not right now. Can't you see I am busy?

Helper: It will only take a minute to open the gift. Come on, it's incredible!

Leader: I can't, I told you that I am busy. How incredible can it really be?

Helper: It will change your life forever!

Leader: I don't believe it.

Helper: Honestly, it will not only change your life, but it will save your life! Please, open it! I went through so much to give you this gift. More than you'll ever know. Please take this gift!

Leader: Like I said, I am busy.

Helper: *(Walk away very sad with your head hanging down, looking back a few times- as if you are heartbroken)*

41

Leader: *(Address the kids with the following sample questions. Be sure to include some of your own! Allow time for response.)*

Sample Questions:

- If you knew a gift could change your life, would you open it?

- Why would you open the gift?

- Do you have any unwrapped gifts at home?

- If you worked hard to make somebody a gift & they never unwrapped it, how would that make you feel?

♥   ♥   ♥   ♥   ♥   ♥   ♥   ♥

Jesus was God's gift to the world. Jesus was God's gift to you. Remember, Romans 6:23 "The wages of sin is death, but the GIFT of God is eternal life through CHRIST JESUS our Lord." God has given us the gift of life. God has given you a way to be washed clean of all your sins, & to live forever in heaven with Him. This gift is Jesus.

Jesus, God's Son, was nailed to a cross & when he was hanging upon that cross, He took the sins of the world upon Him. Jesus paid the price for the sins of the past, present, & the future. Jesus died for your sins. That was God's gift to you. Now all you have to do to be washed clean of those sins is accept the gift God gave you. All you have to do is accept Jesus to be your Lord & savior & do your best to turn away from sin, & follow God. Jesus is the only way to heaven. If you do not accept Jesus, it is like leaving a gift that could save your life unwrapped.

Prepare for your altar call. Allow time for the Holy Spirit to come & have His way in your service. Allow ample time for the Spirit to move.

Royalty in a Far Off Land

Imagine that you belonged to a mighty kingdom, & your father was the richest king in all the land. Since your father is this mighty king, you are entitled to all his kingdom has to offer. All the benefits, all your father's riches, all his power belong to you.

Now imagine that you didn't live in the same kingdom as your father because you were visiting a far off land. Even though you belong to a mighty kingdom, you are not recognized as a prince or a princess because you are living in a different land. You are not living in your father's kingdom.

Do you know this is how it is how it really is for us? God is the mightiest king of all. He is the King above all other kings. God's kingdom is not on earth where we live. God's kingdom is in heaven. If we want to become a part of God's kingdom, & enjoy all the riches of heaven, then we need to accept Jesus, God's one & only son as our Lord.

Jesus left his kingdom in heaven, & came to earth to die for your sins. Jesus paid the price for your sins so you wouldn't have to. If you want to be a part of God's kingdom, then you must accept Jesus into your heart & turn from your sin.

The Bible tells us in 1 Peter, Chapter 2 that you are chosen by God, you were made to be a part of a *royal* priesthood. We are strangers to this world. We do not belong to this world which is full of sin. We can, if we want, choose to belong to this world, or we can choose Jesus & become a part of God's Holy Royal Kingdom.

But you are a chosen people, a royal priesthood, a holy nation, a people belonging to God, that you may declare the praises of him who called you out of darkness into his wonderful light... Dear friends, I urge you, as aliens & strangers in the world, to abstain from sinful desires, which war against your soul. Live such good lives among the pagans that, though they accuse you of doing wrong, they may see your good deeds & glorify God on the day he visits us. 1 Peter 2:9-12

Continue the message into the altar call. Put heavy emphasis on the unconditional love that God has for them. God meets us right where we are & immediately accepts us into His kingdom. The mightiest king, the creator of all is longing & waiting for us to accept Him.

Through the Fire

You will need: A white cotton rag or handkerchief, rubbing alcohol, water, bowl, lighter or matches, tongs, metal bucket or stockpot, fire extinguisher & large bucket of water.

Here's what ya do: Fill a bowl with 3 parts rubbing alcohol & 1 part water. Have your rag soaking & completely saturated in the mixture just prior to the lessons.

♥   ♥   ♥   ♥   ♥   ♥   ♥   ♥

If it seems like a lot of bad things have happened to you in your life, or if your life has been really hard, it is because the devil knows that the plan that God has for your life is so big & so important that he wants to try to do everything he can to turn you away from God, destroy your relationship with God, & destroy you! But, if you believe in God & you accept Jesus into your heart, then nothing the devil, or anyone else can do will be able to destroy you. Your life might still be hard, you will still have troubles, but God will be right there with you in the midst of it all, & He will see you through. Let me demonstrate.

Just because we are Christians does not mean we don't have problems. In fact, God said we would have problems, but He also said that He would always be there for us. He will never leave us or forsake us. No matter how big the problem, God will always see us through.

When we become Christians, this makes the devil very angry, & so he begins his attack!

- *Before you say "attack," pick the rag up with the tongs. Make sure the rag is positioned over metal bucket. When you say "attack" set the handkerchief on fire.*

As long as we have God in our life, we can go through these problems which are life's fiery trials. It may get really hot at times, but we won't get burned. We will go through the fire with God's Holy Spirit inside of us, & come out on the other side unmarked & fully intact!

Hold the handkerchief over the bucket until the fire burns out. The handkerchief will be white & unmarked by the flames. If you need to, you can drop it in the metal bucket or stockpot & let it burn down there.

Great Commission

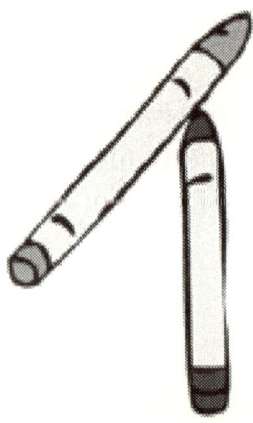

Crafts

Eternity Bracelet

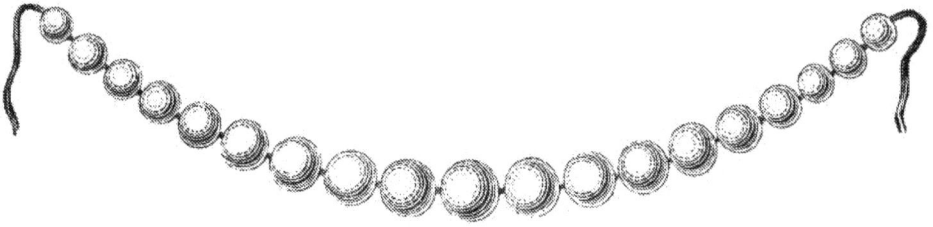

Refer to lesson "Color Me His" on page 30 while working on this project.

Simply string colored beads in the following order:

Black– Our sin

Red – Christ's blood

White – Washed clean

Blue – Baptism

Green – Growing in God

Gold – Heaven

Once the ends of the bracelet are tied together it will form a circle that never ends. It continues forever just like we will live forever with Jesus for eternity.

You can buy beads & string at almost any craft store or online at www.orientaltrading.com

Eternity Necklace with Cross

Follow the directions on the previous page & insert a cross between the white & blue beads.

You can find crosses for beading at your local craft store or online at www.orientaltrading.com

*Tip Tiny hands work better with larger beads & wider holes.

Salvation Rainbow for Tiny Hands

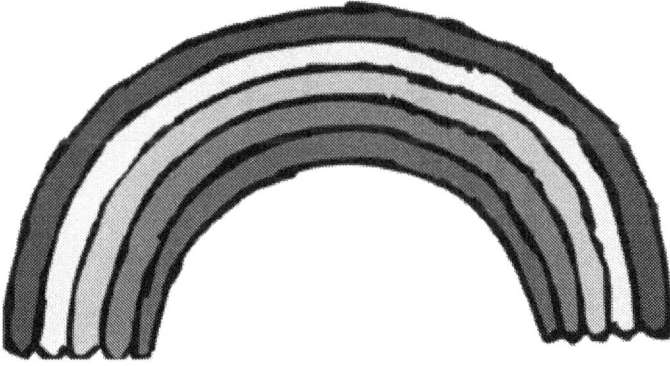

While the big kids are having fun with their crafts, the tiniest hands can learn about Jesus while making a rainbow with finger-paints.

Make sure to have plenty of paper for your little artists. White butcher paper is very economical & easy to pack.

This craft is perfect for the toddlers in your group.

Use the finger-paint recipe on the following page for economical & easy to travel colors.

Finger-paint Recipe

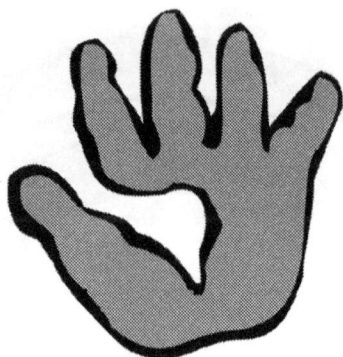

1 cup cornstarch

6 Tablespoons sugar

4 cups water

Food Coloring

Mix cornstarch, sugar, & water. Separate mix into containers. Add a drop of desired food coloring to each container & mix. Mix colors to create additional colors.

Check Lists

&

Organizing Helps

On the following pages you will find reproducible premade & blank charts & checklists. Use these charts to assign jobs, easily organize tasks, & keep track of responsibilities.

Handout the charts to everyone in your group so each person knows exactly who is responsible for what. This helps to avoid common misunderstandings.

When assigning jobs, make sure each person knows exactly what they are responsible for. NEVER ASSUME anything. Give clear & precise instructions, especially where it matters most.

Using charts & checklists makes it easy to see at a glance what is already done & what still needs to be accomplished. You can use colored highlighters to highlight the tasks that are completed & also to make note of the ones that need special attention.

Name:	Task:	Items:	Contact: